Contents

Wear the Shirt with Pride	4
Football Crazy	7
Forever	9
Cold Keeper	11
Wembley	13
Great Save	14
Goal!	17
Snow Joke	18

Wear the Shirt with Pride

Wear the shirt
Feel the pride
Passion burning deep inside.
On the team ... running free
Nowhere you would rather be.

Wear the shirt with pride.

Come on

Wear the shirt with pride.

Football Crazy

Football drives me crazy.

Before every game
I feel sick with fear.
I don't get butterflies
I get huge golden eagles
Soaring round inside me
Like a swirling winter wind.

Yes football drives me crazy …

So how come I love it so much?

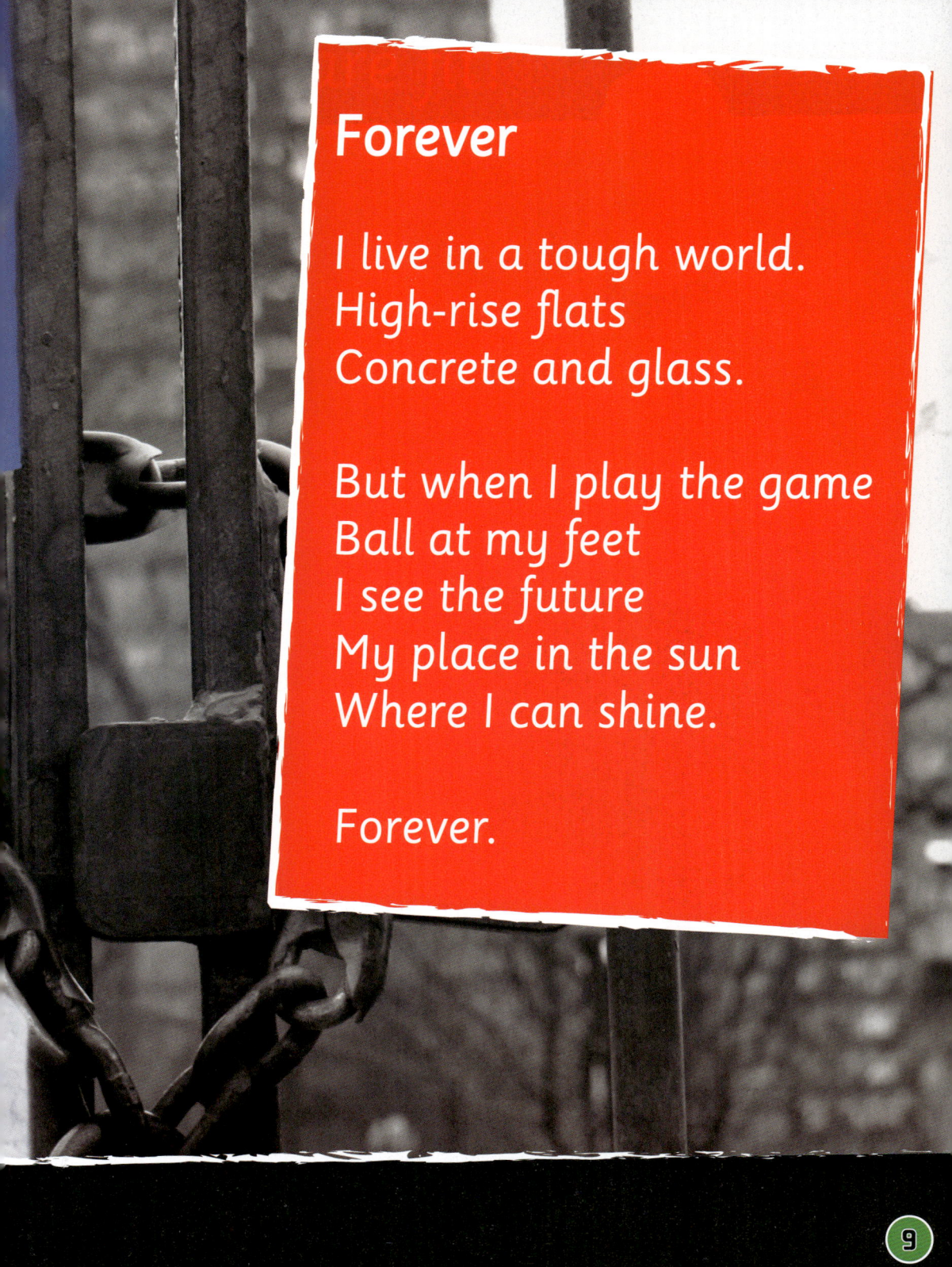

Forever

I live in a tough world.
High-rise flats
Concrete and glass.

But when I play the game
Ball at my feet
I see the future
My place in the sun
Where I can shine.

Forever.

Cold Keeper

I'm a keeper for
The best team in town.
To tell the truth
It gets me down.

I'd love to dive
And save a shot.
Defending corners
Would be hot.

But we win every
Game with ease.
That's why I stand around
And freeze!

Wembley

Wembley is my dream.
One day I will win the Cup

Climb those famous steps …

Great Save

I face the striker
For the vital penalty.
My heart beats faster.

He hits his shot hard.
I dive full length and save it.
Never felt so good.

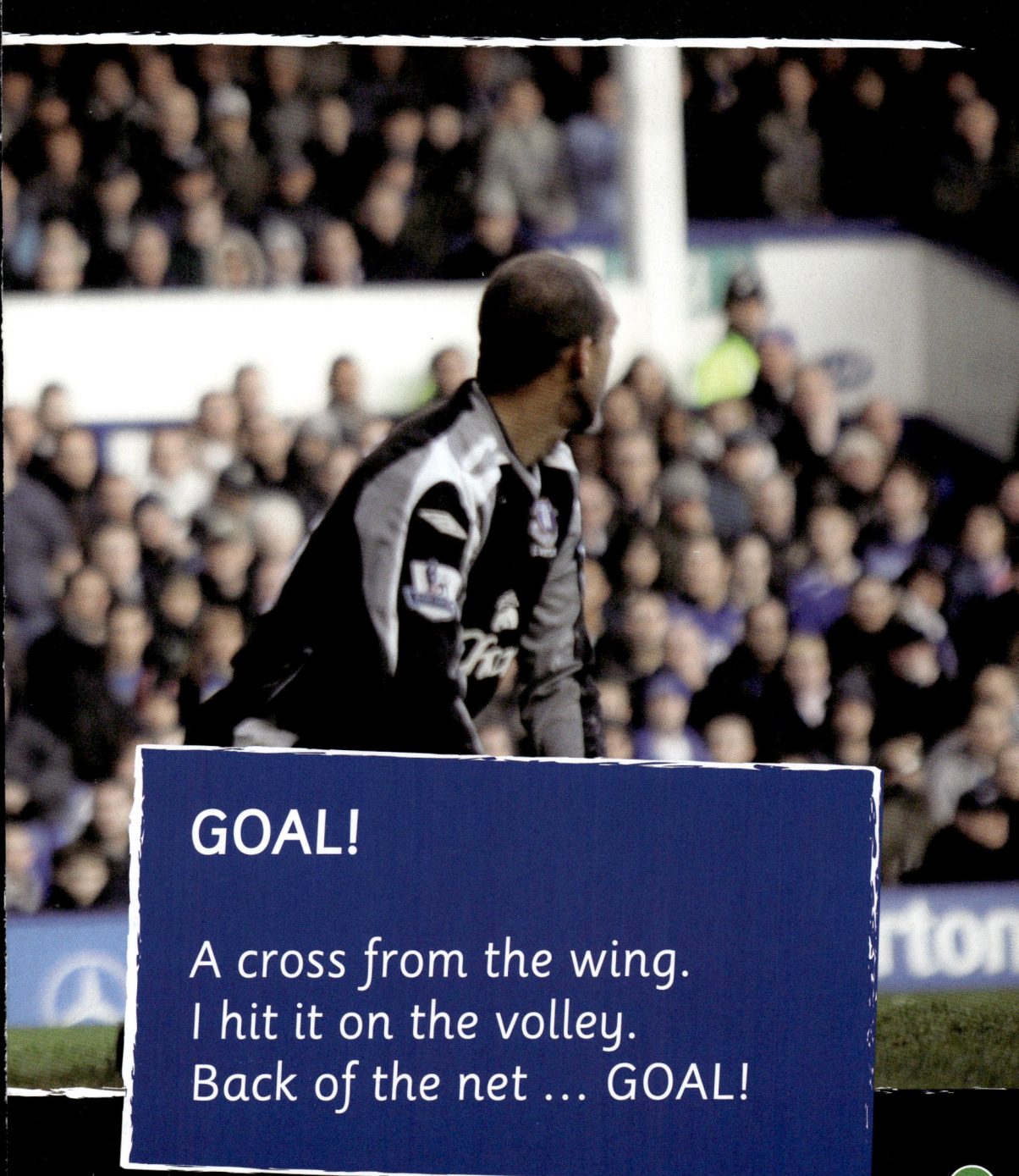

GOAL!

A cross from the wing.
I hit it on the volley.
Back of the net ... GOAL!

Snow Joke

Football in the snow,
- it seemed like fun.
I'm not smiling now,
- the snowmen won!